FABLE & FLORA

COPYRIGHT © 2024 JACQUELINE BUTTON
PUBLISHED BY FABLE & FAUNA
ALL RIGHTS RESERVED. NO PART OF THIS PUBLICATION MAY BE REPRODUCED, STORED IN A RETRIEVAL SYSTEM, OR TRANSMITTED IN ANY FORM OR BY ANY MEANS— ELECTRONIC, MECHANICAL, PHOTOCOPYING, RECORDING, OR OTHERWISE—WITHOUT THE PRIOR WRITTEN PERMISSION OF THE PUBLISHER, EXCEPT FOR BRIEF QUOTATIONS USED IN REVIEWS OR ARTICLES.
THIS BOOK IS INTENDED FOR INSPIRATIONAL AND PERSONAL DEVELOPMENT PURPOSES ONLY AND IS NOT A SUBSTITUTE FOR PROFESSIONAL ADVICE, THERAPY, OR MEDICAL CARE. THE AUTHOR AND PUBLISHER MAKE NO GUARANTEES REGARDING THE OUTCOME OF USING THE SUGGESTIONS OR AFFIRMATIONS INCLUDED.
ISBN NUMBER]979-8-218-56326-4

# FABLE & FLORA

# I THINK I'LL CHANGE MY MIND

DAILY AFFIRMATIONS FOR OPTIMAL
SUBCONSCIOUS PROGRAMMING
FOR AGES 0-1000

## A NOTE FROM THE AUTHOR

YOU ARE AMAZING, YOU ARE POWERFUL, YOU ARE BEAUTIFUL, AND YOUR THOUGHTS, WORDS, AND EMOTIONS REALLY DO MATTER. THEY ARE LITERAL MATTER. WAVES ECHOING OUT INTO THE UNIVERSE, YOUR GIFT OF CREATION FROM GOD. LET THIS BOOK EMPOWER YOU TO INTENTIONALLY CREATE AN AMAZING WORLD FROM THE INSIDE OUT.

I LOVE YOU. I LOVE YOU. I LOVE YOU

## DEDICATED TO THE ONES I LOVE

DALLAS, THANK YOU FOR WAKING ME UP.
TAYLOR, THANK YOU FOR BEING MY LIGHT.
IRIS, THANK YOU FOR BEING MY RAINBOW.
ADA, THANK YOU FOR BEING MY COMFORT.
SUNNY, THANK YOU FOR BEING MY HOPE.
NICK, THANK YOU FOR ALL OF THE ABOVE AND SO MUCH MORE.
MOM, DAD, JUDY- I LOVE YOU.

# PROGRAM YOUR MIND

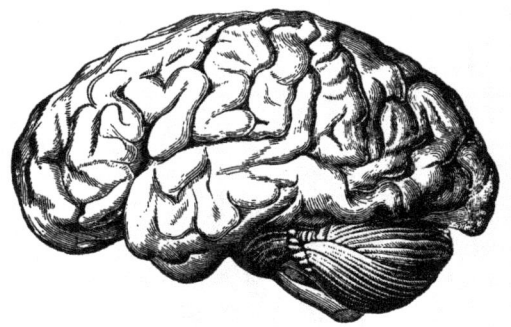

THE POWER TO CREATE THE LIFE OF YOUR DREAMS
LIES WITHIN YOUR SUBCONSCIOUS MIND —
A MIND THAT IS ENDLESSLY ADAPTABLE,
CAPABLE OF CHANGE THROUGH NEUROPLASTICITY.
THE WORDS YOU SPEAK,
THE EMOTIONS YOU FEEL,
AND THE THOUGHTS YOU THINK
ARE THE HOLY TRINITY OF WHAT SHAPES AND SEASONS
YOUR HUMAN EXPERIENCE,
UNCONSCIOUS BELIEFS QUIETLY RESIDE
WITHIN YOUR SUBCONSCIOUS MIND.
THESE BELIEFS INFLUENCE YOUR DAILY LIFE.
YOUR BRAIN CAN REWIRE ITSELF AND THESE BELIEFS
CAN BE TRANSFORMED AND RENEWED.
BY PRACTICING INTENTIONAL AFFIRMATIONS,
VISUALIZATION,
AND FOCUSED FEELING,
YOU ACTIVATE THE BRAIN'S THETA AND ALPHA STATES
—THE OPTIMAL FREQUENCIES FOR DEEP SUBCONSCIOUS
PROGRAMMING. THETA WAVES (4–8 HZ) OPEN THE DOOR
TO INTUITION, CREATIVITY, AND DEEP LEARNING,
WHILE ALPHA WAVES (8–13 HZ) BRING RELAXED
ALERTNESS,
ALLOWING YOUR SUBCONSCIOUS TO ABSORB NEW,
EMPOWERING BELIEFS. WITH DAILY PRACTICE,
ESPECIALLY IN THE MORNING AND EVENING,
WHEN YOUR MIND NATURALLY DRIFTS INTO THESE
STATES,
SPEAK THESE WORDS ALOUD, VISUALIZE THEIR MEANING,
AND MOST IMPORTANTLY — FEEL THEM AS TRUTH.
ENGAGE ALL YOUR SENSES,
IMAGINE THIS NEW REALITY FULLY ALIVE.
READ THEM TO YOURSELF, TO A CHILD, TO YOUR LOVED
ONES — AND TOGETHER, LET'S BEGIN
TO CREATE LITTLE POCKETS OF HEAVEN
RIGHT HERE ON EARTH.

# INSPIRATION AND REVELATIONS

"MAN IS LOOKING EVERYWHERE FOR GOD, NOT KNOWING THAT WHEN HE SAYS 'I AM' HE IS ANNOUNCING THE PRESENCE OF THE LIVING GOD WITHIN HIMSELF. THIS IS CALLED THE MASTER SECRET OF THE AGES, SOMETIMES REFERRED TO AS THE LOST WORD. 'I AM' MEANS BEING, LIFE, AWARENESS, THE PRESENCE OF GOD IN MAN. IT IS THE NAMELESS ONE.
IN ANCIENT TIMES, THE SECRET WAS GIVEN ONLY TO THE INITIATED, NEVER TO THE PROFANE, BECAUSE THE ANCIENT SEERS SAID WITH THIS KNOWLEDGE, OR AWARENESS, A MAN CAN RISE TO THE HEIGHTS OF SPIRITUAL ILLUMINATION, OR HE CAN SINK TO THE DEPTHS OF DEGRADATION. HENCE, IT WAS GIVEN ONLY TO THOSE WHO WERE SPIRITUALLY AWAKENED AND STOOD THE TESTS THAT WERE GIVEN THEM."

-JOSEPH MURPHY
*YOU CAN CHANGE YOUR WHOLE LIFE*
*1961*

# THOUGHTS ARE THINGS

"WHATSOEVER THINGS ARE JUST,

WHATSOEVER THINGS ARE PURE,

WHATSOEVER THINGS ARE LOVELY,

WHATSOEVER THINGS ARE OF GOOD REPORT;

IF THERE BE ANY VIRTUE,

AND IF THERE BE ANY PRAISE,

THINK ONLY ON THESE THINGS."

PHILIPPIANS 4:8

# JUST FOR TODAY

I AM RESPONSIBLE

I AM RESPONSIBLE
FOR MY HAPPINESS

I AM FINDING WAYS
TO CREATE HAPPINESS

I AM HAPPY FOR MYSELF
I AM HAPPY FOR OTHERS

AND SHARE IT FAR AND WIDE

# JUST FOR TODAY

I AM TAKING CARE OF MY BODY

I HAVE A ROUTINE FOR SELF CARE

# JUST FOR TODAY

I KNOW MY BODY
IS MY TEMPLE

IT IS THE HOUSE
OF MY SOUL

I TAKE ACTIONS
THAT REFLECT
MY REVERENCE
AND
RESPECT
FOR MY BODY

# JUST FOR TODAY

I WILL MOVE

AND

S T R E T C H

AND

NOURISH

MY BODY

# JUST FOR TODAY

I AM

STRENGTHENING

MY

MIND

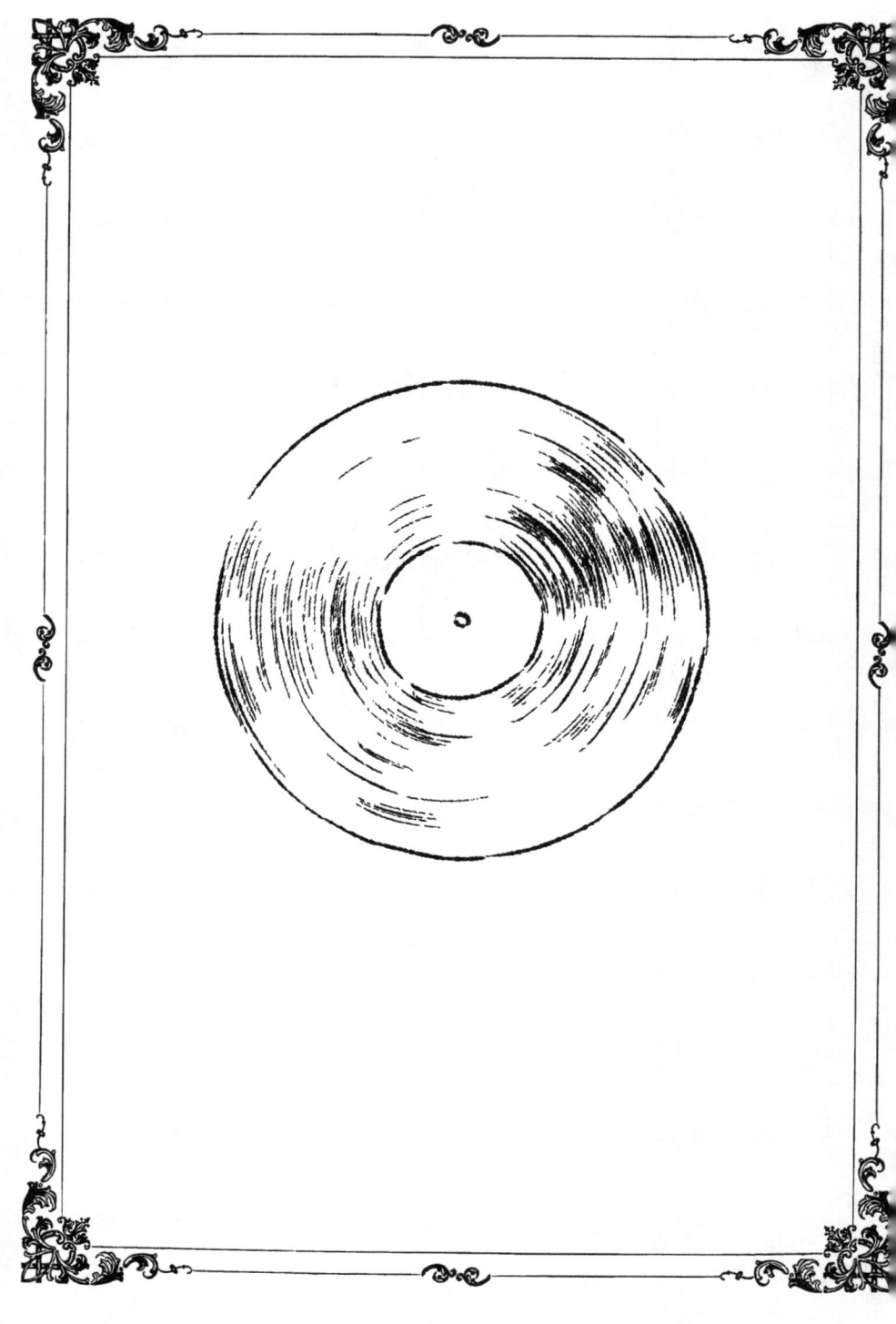

## JUST FOR TODAY

I AM

OBSERVING MY THOUGHTS

AND DISCARDING

THAT

WHICH

DOES NOT SERVE ME

WITH LOVE AND GRATITUDE

## JUST FOR TODAY

I ALLOW
GOOD THINGS TO HAPPEN

I ALLOW LOVE
TO FLOW INTO MY LIFE

I ALLOW
AND WELCOME
MIRACLES TO SURPRISE
AND DELIGHT ME

# JUST FOR TODAY

I AM

DIRECTING MY ATTENTION

THOUGHTFULLY

CAREFULLY

AND

INTENTIONALLY

# JUST FOR TODAY

I AM GIVING

ATTENTION

ONLY

TO THAT WHICH

MOVES ME

FORWARD

I AM FOCUSED
ON
MY HIGHEST PATH

I WILL CREATE
A LOVELY SCENE
WITH MY IMAGINATION

# JUST FOR TODAY

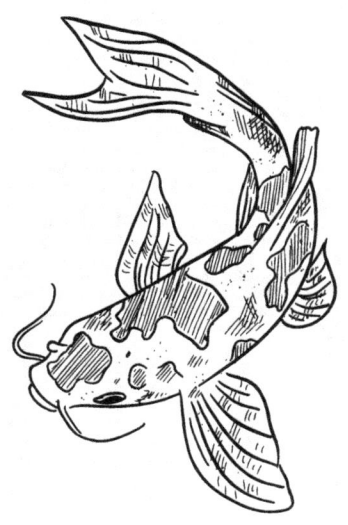

I AM

EXERCISING

MY

SOUL

# JUST FOR TODAY

I AM GRATEFUL.

I AM GRATEFUL FOR THE
POWER OF CHOICE.
I HONOR THIS POWER
BY CHOOSING TO
SEE THE GOOD
IN THE WORLD.

# JUST FOR TODAY

I AM

FINDING WAYS

TO SERVE OTHERS

WITHOUT

EXPECTING

ANYTHING IN RETURN

# JUST FOR TODAY

I AM
GROUNDED
IN MY BODY
I AM
GROUNDED
IN THE
PRESENT

# JUST FOR TODAY

I AM

ALLOWING OTHERS

TO BE

AS THEY ARE

WITH

LOVE AND ACCEPTANCE

# JUST FOR TODAY

I AM

DOING A FEW THINGS

THAT I DON'T REALLY WANT TO

BUT I KNOW I HAVE TO DO

**WITHOUT** COMPLAINING

# JUST FOR TODAY

I TAKE PRIDE

IN MY

APPEARANCE

I AM

PRESENTING MYSELF

TO THE WORLD

WITH GREAT CARE AND

PURPOSE

# JUST FOR TODAY

I CHOOSE

MY WORDS

CAREFULLY AND SPEAK

WITH

INTENTION

# JUST FOR TODAY

I TALK

A LITTLE LESS

AND

I LISTEN

A LITTLE MORE

WITH AN OPEN MIND

# JUST FOR TODAY

I SHARPEN MY

FOCUS TO

MY OWN

SELF IMPROVEMENT

# JUST FOR TODAY

I AM

PRESENT

I EMBRACE

MY OPPORTUNITIES

WITH A HUMBLE

AND GRATEFUL

HEART

# JUST FOR TODAY

I AM

TAKING STEPS

TOWARDS MY

GOALS

AND

EMBRACING THE JOURNEY

# JUST FOR TODAY

I WILL

MAKE AN EFFORT

TO SEEK TO

UNDERSTAND RATHER

THAN TO BE

UNDERSTOOD

# JUST FOR TODAY

I AM

FINDING

BEAUTY IN THE
MUNDANE

AND

CREATIVITY IN
BOREDOM

# JUST FOR TODAY

I AM FILLED WITH GRATITUDE

I AM USING MY VOICE TO SPEAK KINDNESS AND LOVE

MY THOUGHTS ARE POSITIVE

ANYTHING NOT IN ALIGNMENT WITH MY HIGHEST PATH FLOATS THROUGH MY MIND LIKE A SHIP IN THE NIGHT

# JUST FOR TODAY

I AM CALM

I AM CENTERED

I AM CONFIDENT

I REST IN THE KNOWING THAT EVERYTHING IS HAPPENING FOR ME IN THE MOST BEAUTIFUL WAY

# JUST FOR TODAY

I AM ABLE

TO

SEE

THE BEAUTY

IN THE DANCE

OF LIFE

WHEN MY JOURNEY

UNFOLDS

IN UNEXPECTED WAYS

# JUST FOR TODAY

I COUNT MY MANY BLESSINGS

I BRING MY BEST

SELF FORWARD

IN ALL OF MY

THOUGHTS

FEELINGS

AND

ACTIONS

# JUST FOR TODAY

I SIT IN SILENCE

I QUIET MY MIND

I APPRECIATE

THE RHYTHM OF MY BREATH

THE BEAT OF MY HEART

AND THE LIFE THAT I AM

I CONNECT WITH ALL THAT IS

# JUST FOR TODAY

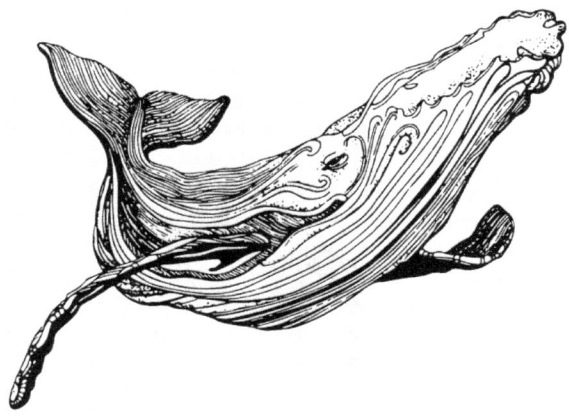

I AM BRAVE

WHEN THE WORLD

TELLS ME TO BE AFRAID

I EMBODY COURAGE AND HOPE

I AM

NOT AFRAID

TO ENJOY WHAT IS BEAUTIFUL

AND HAVE FAITH IN THE GOOD

# JUST FOR TODAY

I AM NOT AFRAID

TO GIVE LOVE

AND KNOW I AM LOVED

# JUST FOR TODAY

I AM RELEASING

ANY ATTACHMENT

TO THE VALUE I HAVE ASSIGNED

TO THE THOUGHTS AND OPINIONS

OF OTHERS

# JUST FOR TODAY

I FOCUS ON OBSERVING

AND ADJUSTING MY OWN

THOUGHTS ABOUT

MYSELF

# JUST FOR TODAY

I AM ALIGNED IN THOUGHT

I AM ALIGNED IN ACTION

THE WORDS I SPEAK ARE IN ALIGNMENT WITH MY HIGHEST PATH

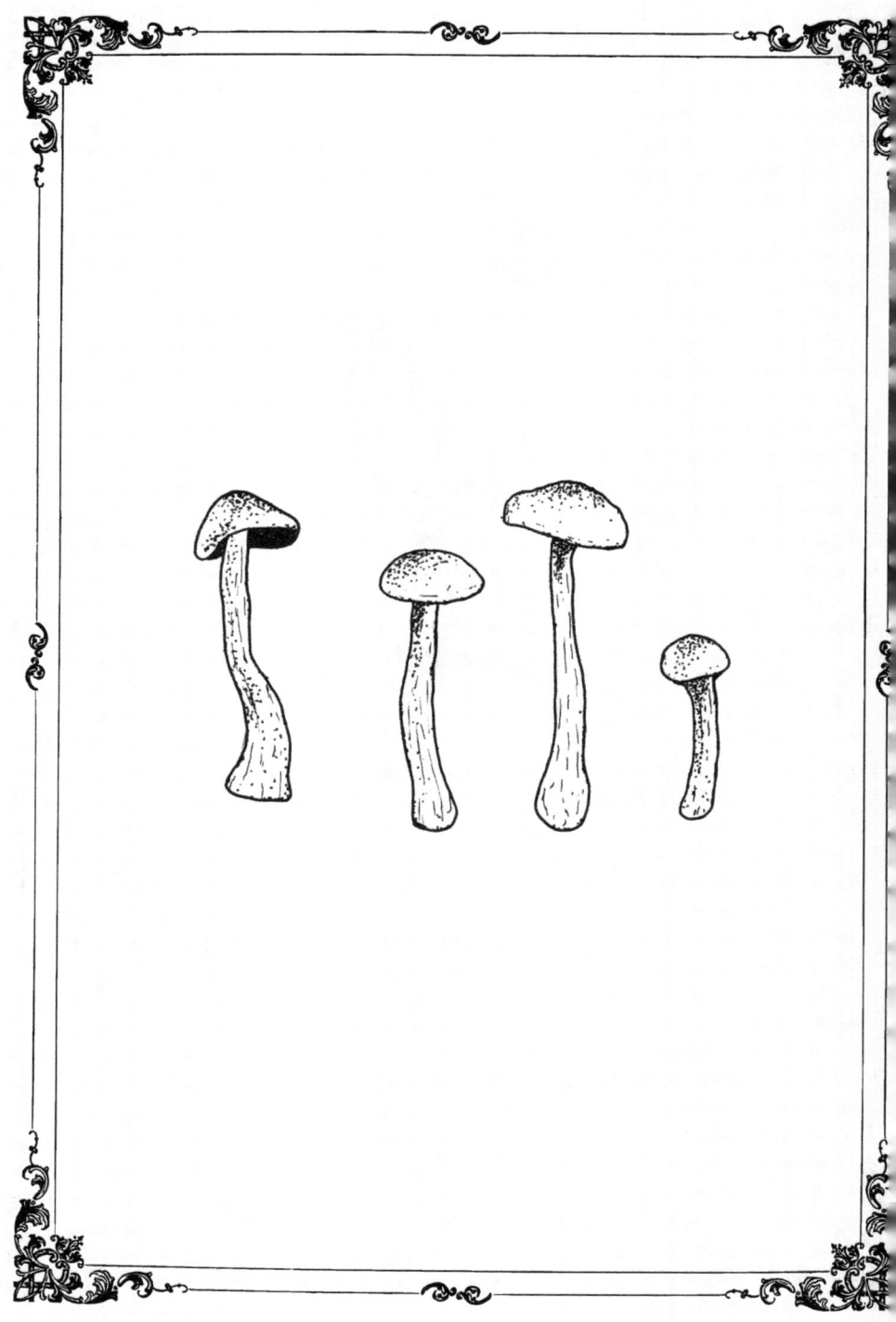

# JUST FOR TODAY

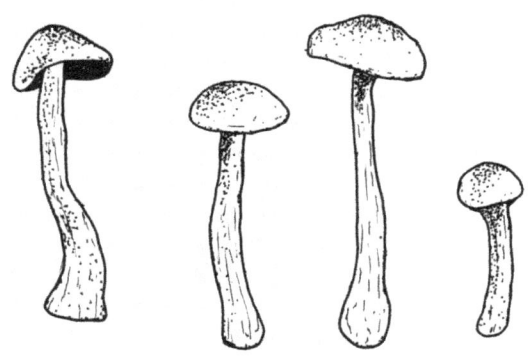

I FIND

STRENGTH

COMFORT

AND

POWER

IN THE FACT THAT

MY OPINIONS ABOUT MYSELF

ARE THE ONLY

ONES THAT MATTER

# JUST FOR TODAY

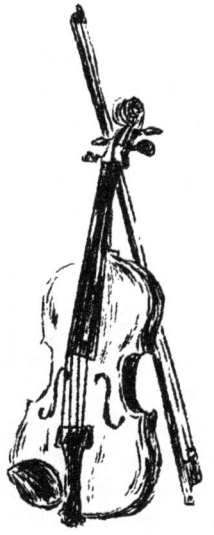

I WILL BRING MY BEST SELF
FORWARD


I AM HUMBLE


I AM GRATEFUL
FOR THIS NOW MOMENT

# JUST FOR TODAY

I AM WILLING
AND EXCITED
TO LEARN SOMETHING NEW

I SAVOR
THE SATISFACTION
OF A JOB WELL DONE

# JUST FOR TODAY

I AM OBSERVING ME

I OBSERVE MY THOUGHTS WITHOUT JUDGEMENT

I OBSERVE MY ACTIONS

I OBSERVE MY HABITS

I OBSERVE THE PEOPLE IN MY LIFE

I AM UNATTACHED AWARENESS

# JUST FOR TODAY

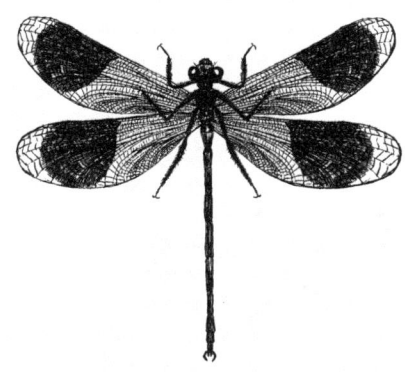

I

AM

WORTHY

BECAUSE

I

EXIST

# JUST FOR TODAY

I AM

SPEAKING

WITH

LOVE

# JUST FOR TODAY

I AM

USING MY

WORDS

TO CREATE

LOVE

# JUST FOR TODAY

I AM

FEELING

AND RADIATING

LOVE

AND GRATITUDE

# JUST FOR TODAY

I AM USING MY IMAGINATION

TO CREATE

THE FEELING,

THE KNOWING, AND THE

VISION OF MY PERFECT WORLD

# JUST FOR TODAY

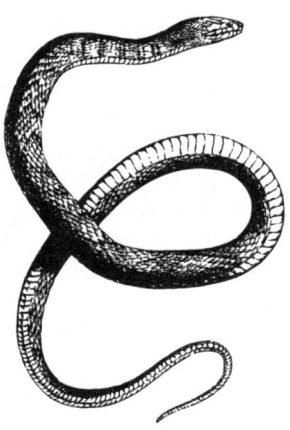

I AM
SEEING EVERYONE

AND EVERYTHING

THROUGH THE EYES

OF UNCONDITIONAL

LOVE

# JUST FOR TODAY

I KNOW

EVERYONE HAS A STORY

I TREAT EVERYONE

WITH COMPASSION

AND KINDNESS

# JUST FOR TODAY

I KNOW I
AM APPRECIATED

I MATTER

AND

I AM LOVED

# JUST FOR TODAY

I AM GOING TO PLAY

CREATE

AND HAVE FUN

# JUST FOR TODAY

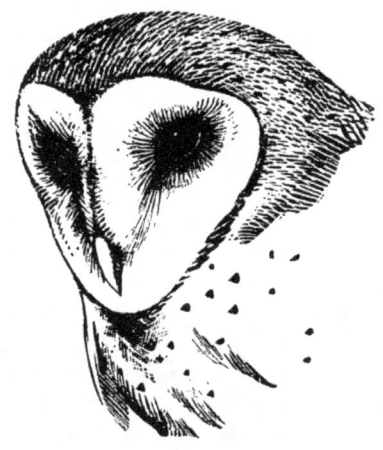

I DREAM A DREAM OF HEAVEN

I DREAM OF A WORLD OF PEACE,
LOVE
AND HARMONY.

I BECOME THAT PEACE.

I BECOME HEAVEN ON EARTH.

EVERYONE THAT ENTERS

MY FIELD FINDS

A SENSE OF HOME AND BELONGING.

# JUST FOR TODAY

I FEEL

HAPPY

JOYOUS

AND

FREE

# JUST FOR TODAY

I AM IN LOVE
WITH
MY LIFE

MY ABUNDANCE
OVERFLOWS
INTO THE CUPS OF THOSE
AROUND ME

# JUST FOR TODAY

I AM

UNCONDITIONAL

LOVE

I LOVE WITHOUT
CONDITIONS

# JUST FOR TODAY

# JUST FOR TODAY

# JUST FOR TODAY

# JUST FOR TODAY

# JUST FOR TODAY

# JUST FOR TODAY

# JUST FOR TODAY

# JUST FOR TODAY

# JUST FOR TODAY

# JUST FOR TODAY

# JUST FOR TODAY

# JUST FOR TODAY

# JUST FOR TODAY

# JUST FOR TODAY

# JUST FOR TODAY

# JUST FOR TODAY

_____

_____

_____

_____

_____

_____

_____

_____

_____

_____

# JUST FOR TODAY

# JUST FOR TODAY

# JUST FOR TODAY

# JUST FOR TODAY

# JUST FOR TODAY

# JUST FOR TODAY

# JUST FOR TODAY

# JUST FOR TODAY

# JUST FOR TODAY

# JUST FOR TODAY

# JUST FOR TODAY

# JUST FOR TODAY

# JUST FOR TODAY

# JUST FOR TODAY

# JUST FOR TODAY

# JUST FOR TODAY

# JUST FOR TODAY

# JUST FOR TODAY

# JUST FOR TODAY

# JUST FOR TODAY

# JUST FOR TODAY

_____
_____
_____
_____
_____
_____
_____
_____
_____

# JUST FOR TODAY

# JUST FOR TODAY

# JUST FOR TODAY

# JUST FOR TODAY

# JUST FOR TODAY

_____
_____
_____
_____
_____
_____
_____
_____
_____

# JUST FOR TODAY

# JUST FOR TODAY

# JUST FOR TODAY

# JUST FOR TODAY

# JUST FOR TODAY

# JUST FOR TODAY

# JUST FOR TODAY

# JUST FOR TODAY

# JUST FOR TODAY

_____
_____
_____
_____
_____
_____
_____
_____
_____
_____

# JUST FOR TODAY

# JUST FOR TODAY

# JUST FOR TODAY

# JUST FOR TODAY

# JUST FOR TODAY

www.ingramcontent.com/pod-product-compliance
Lightning Source LLC
Chambersburg PA
CBHW070330010526
44107CB00004B/475